EASTER

An Easy-Read Holiday Book

EASTER

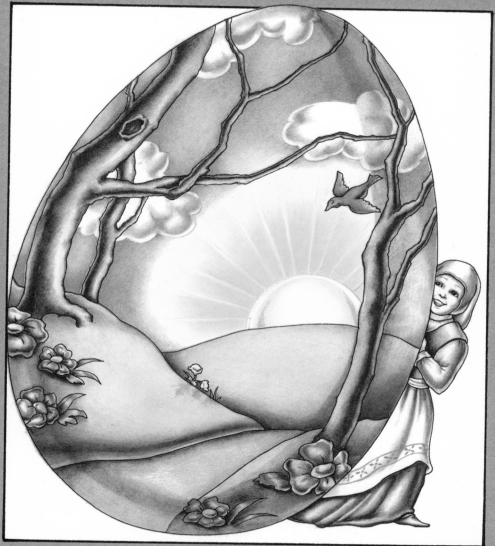

by Cass R. Sandak

illustrations by Diana Uehlinger

FRANKLIN WATTS
New York/London/Toronto/Sydney
1980

For Larky and the kids

R.L. 2.9 Spache Revised Formula

Library of Congress Cataloging in Publication Data

Sandak, Cass R
  Easter.

  (An Easy-read holiday book)
  Includes index.
  SUMMARY: Presents the history and customs of
  Easter.
  1. Easter — Juvenile literature. [1. Easter]
I. Uehlinger, Diana. II. Title. III. Series: Easy-read
holiday book.
GT4935.S23   394.2′68283   80-10510
ISBN 0-531-04148-4

Easter is a time of joy. The Easter season celebrates the coming of spring. As a religious holiday, Easter Sunday celebrates Christ's **resurrection** (rezz-ah-RECK-shun). Christians believe that Jesus Christ rose from the dead on Easter Sunday nearly two thousand years ago. Easter means new life—a new beginning. It is a time for all people to be happy.

In many places, cold weather keeps people inside most of the winter. In the spring, life begins again outdoors. Birds sing in the trees. Flowers bloom. Baby chicks hatch from their eggs. All these things show the wonders of spring.

In the spring the sun rises earlier and earlier each day. Days grow longer and become warmer. Because of this, long ago people of different races and religions held spring festivals.

Easter is our spring festival. No one knows for sure where the name Easter comes from. Some people think that it comes from the direction East, where the sun rises.

The Anglo-Saxons were people who lived in England more than a thousand years ago. They called a whole month **Eastur-monath** (eh-YAW-stir MOH-nawth). This means the "month of the growing sun." It was about the same month we call April. The name April comes from a Latin word that means "to open." April is the month when buds swell and open. We open our doors and go out into the fresh air.

Christian people in many countries celebrate Easter Sunday and sometimes Easter Monday. Some schools are closed for all of Easter week. In many countries and in parts of the United States, Good Friday and Easter Monday are legal holidays. In these places, banks and other businesses may be closed.

Easter is the oldest Christian holiday. It has been a church festival since the time of Jesus' earliest followers. Early churches could not agree on a date for Easter. In the year 325, however, the **Council of Nicaea** (ny-SEE-uh) chose the way we find when Easter comes.

The date of Easter changes from year to year. But it is always on a Sunday. It may come as early as March 22 or as late as April 25. Easter may be on any Sunday between these two dates.

The date of Easter depends on the moon and the sun and on the date of the **vernal equinox** (VUR-null EE-kwee-nocks). Vernal means spring. Equinox comes from two Latin words that mean "equal night."

The equinox is a day when there are the same number of hours of sunlight and of darkness. This happens twice each year, once in the spring and once in the autumn. The usual date for the spring equinox is March 21. But the actual time when day and night are the same length may come a day or two earlier or later.

Easter is always the Sunday following the first full moon on or after the vernal equinox.

After the vernal equinox, days get longer as the sun rises earlier and sets later. The Anglo-Saxons called the spring season **Lenctentid** (LENG-ten-teed), which means "the time of lengthening." We take our word **Lent** from this Old English word for spring.

Lent is the time of year that leads up to Easter. It begins on Ash Wednesday, when many Christians go to church services. Often at these services the priest or minister uses ashes to make a cross on each person's forehead. The ashes come from palm branches that have been burned.

Because the date of Easter changes, Ash Wednesday also comes on a different date each year.

Lent is a time of fasting. Fasting is a word that has two meanings. It can mean eating no food. At breakfast, we **break** the **fast** that we have kept all night. Or fasting can mean eating lightly.

Many people think fasting is good for their health. Or they may fast for religious reasons. For hundreds of years, most people did not eat meat, cheese, butter, fat, and eggs during Lent. Nowadays we often give up something we enjoy, like candy or sweets.

Fasts during Lent probably began from a need to make food supplies last longer. In earlier times, very little food from the last harvest was left by the beginning of spring. It was a good idea to give up some things during this time.

There are forty-six days between Ash Wednesday and Easter. But since Sundays during this time are not fast days, the actual length of Lent is forty days. Lent ends the day before Easter.

In Great Britain, and sometimes in the United States, the few days before Ash Wednesday are called **Shrovetide**. "Shrove" comes from the word "shrift," an old word for a confession. "Tide" means time. In earlier times, people made a confession to their priests before the start of Lent.

Other customs gave their names to each of the days in Shrovetide. The Saturday before Ash Wednesday was once called Egg Saturday. Children went from house to house begging for eggs that had to be eaten before the beginning of Lent. They threw broken dishes at the doors of houses where they didn't get eggs!

The day before Ash Wednesday is still sometimes called Shrove Tuesday. It is also called Pancake Tuesday. In some places, such as Great Britain, it is the custom to make pancakes on this day. Long ago, the eggs and cooking fat for pancakes had to be used up before the start of Lent.

19

In some parts of Europe and South America, Shrovetide is also called **Carnival** (CAR-nuh-vull) time. The word carnival means "farewell to meat." In earlier times, meat was not eaten during Lent.

In France and in French-speaking countries, carnival time is also called **Mardi Gras** (MAR-dee graw). This means "Fat Tuesday" in French. It is the last day to use up cooking fat before Lent begins.

In the United States, Mardi Gras is still held in some cities in the South that were settled by the French. The most famous Mardi Gras celebration is in **New Orleans** (New OR-lee-unz), **Louisiana** (loo-EE-zee-ann-uh). It was first held in the early 1800s. Mardi Gras parades and fancy dress balls end at midnight, when Ash Wednesday begins.

When Lent begins, Christians try to understand Jesus' last days on earth.

The last week of Lent is called Holy Week. In the days leading up to Easter Sunday, Christians remember the story of Christ's death and resurrection.

The Sunday before Easter is called Palm Sunday. Many churches hand out palm branches or little crosses made from palms on this day. This marks the day Jesus came into **Jerusalem** (juh-ROO-sah-lem). His followers waved palm branches to greet him. This was a sign of respect. Jesus had come to the city to celebrate the Jewish Passover.

Passover comes at about the same time as the Christian Holy Week. Passover lasts for eight days. It is one of the most important Jewish holidays. During Passover, Jews remember how Moses led his people out of Egypt, where they were slaves, hundreds of years before the birth of Christ.

During Holy Week, services are held every day
in many churches.

The Thursday of Holy Week is often called
Maundy (MAWN-dee) Thursday. Maundy comes
from a Latin word that means "a command."
Jesus commanded his followers to love one another.

24

Today rulers and religious leaders try to follow the command Jesus made on Maundy Thursday. One way is to help others. At a special service, Queen Elizabeth II of Great Britain gives money to older people from a special basket.

On the first Maundy Thursday, Jesus ate with his friends for the last time. Many artists have painted this meal, which is called the "Last Supper." Later the same evening, Judas, one of Jesus' friends, had him arrested. The next day, Friday, Jesus was brought to trial, though he had done nothing wrong.

The Friday of Holy Week is called Good Friday. This name probably comes from "God's Friday." Christians believe that Jesus was God's son.

On Good Friday, Jesus was nailed to a wooden cross. Several hours later he died. This kind of death is called a **crucifixion** (croo-sih-FICK-shun). Long ago, many people were put to death in this way.

The cross on which Jesus died has become an important sign of the Christian faith. During Lent, some people take part in a devotion called the Stations of the Cross. The fourteen "stations" are prayers and readings about Christ's trial and crucifixion.

After the crucifixion on Good Friday, Jesus' friends put his body in a tomb. The following Sunday morning, three women went to the tomb. There they found an angel who told them that Jesus was gone. He had risen from the dead. This was the first Easter Sunday.

Later, Jesus' friends saw him, spoke with him, and touched him. Then, as people watched, Jesus rose up to heaven.

Church services during Holy Week are serious and quiet. Church bells are not rung between Maundy Thursday and Easter Sunday. Children in some countries are told that the bells have gone to Rome to visit the Pope. The bells then fly back home early Easter morning, bringing the decorated eggs that are left in baskets for the children.

28

In early times, people placed their Easter eggs in grass nests that were made to look like birds' nests. Later, baskets filled with straw took the place of nests. Today, Easter baskets are decorated with ribbons, flowers, and straw. They are filled with eggs, jelly beans, and other Easter sweets. A chocolate rabbit or yellow marshmallow chick is a welcome sight in an Easter basket, especially if you gave up candy or sweets for Lent!

Many Easter customs come from Europe, where eggs have been decorated for hundreds of years. These eggs are said to be brought by the Easter rabbit.

The eggs used for dyeing or painting are usually hens' eggs, or other birds' eggs. But some early people celebrated the beginning of spring by dancing around a pile of snakes' eggs. The people of ancient Persia gave each other eggs dyed red on the first day of spring. The Chinese still present gifts of eggs to the parents of newborn children. Around the world, the egg, like the seed, is a sign of life.

Throughout Eastern and Central Europe, making Easter eggs is taken very seriously. The most elaborate eggs are probably those decorated by people from Poland and from the **Ukraine** (YOU-krane), a part of the Soviet Union. These people call their eggs **pysanki** (pee-SANK-ee), which means "written eggs."

The eggs are decorated in a way that is like writing. A type of pen is used to draw signs and pictures on the eggs with wax. Then the eggs are dyed. The dye will not stay where the wax has been placed. When the dyeing is finished, the wax is melted off and leaves a design.

Other groups have their own ways of making Easter eggs. The Pennsylvania Dutch dye their eggs. Then they scratch the shells with a knife or needle. This scrapes away a little of the dye and makes a lacy white pattern on the shell.

Probably the most beautiful Easter eggs are not real eggs at all! About one hundred years ago, a jeweler named Carl **Fabergé** (fab-ur-ZHAY) lived in Russia. He made eggs out of gold, silver, and jewels. At Easter time, the Russian **Czar** (ZAR) or Emperor gave these eggs as gifts. Almost always the eggs open up and show a surprise—perhaps tiny figures of people and animals.

Museums may have collections of all kinds of beautiful Easter eggs that are more than a hundred years old.

32

Today we may make Easter eggs in a simpler way. Easter tints are often used. These are robins' egg blue, the pale yellow of a newly hatched chick, the purple of violets, or the light green of grass on a spring morning. You may enjoy hanging your Easter eggs on an egg tree. The Pennsylvania Dutch set up the first egg trees.

According to folklore, a German duchess started the custom of hiding brightly decorated eggs. These were said to have been left by the Easter rabbit for the country children. The children then made a game of finding the eggs.

Sometimes the Easter egg hunt is a treasure hunt. The hiding places are given in written clues. The treasure hunt is finished when all the eggs have been found. The person who puts the most eggs into his or her basket wins the game.

In the early 1800s, Dolley Madison, the wife of President James Madison, the fourth president of the United States, began the Easter Egg Roll in Washington, D.C. This event is still held each year on Easter Monday. For about the first fifty years, the Egg Roll took place near the Capitol building. Since the 1860s, it has been held on the White House lawn. Children roll eggs down a hill to see which egg will go the farthest without breaking.

Because Easter marks the rebirth of nature, many of its signs are outdoor things—animals and plants.

The animals we think of most often at Easter are chickens, lambs, and rabbits. The lamb is a sign of good luck at Easter. In many places, cakes and chocolate are made in the shape of a lamb.

Because rabbits give birth to five or six litters of babies each year, they stand for the richness of nature. German settlers brought the idea of the Easter rabbit to the United States in the late 1700s.

Plants and flowers are important parts of Easter. They make nice Easter gifts. Women often wear **orchids** (OR-kidz) or other flowers on Easter Sunday.

Many kinds of bulb flowers bloom in the spring. The flowers seem delicate, but they are hardy and strong. The bulbs lie in the cold ground all winter. Crocuses may bloom even while there is snow on the ground. Daffodils and tulips come later.

Perhaps more than any other flower, lilies stand for Easter. For hundreds of years, religious pictures have shown different kinds of lilies. Lily flowers are shaped like bells or trumpets. They remind people of joyful music. Their sweet smell and simple form seem to stand for everything pure and perfect.

Many countries have traditional Easter foods.
Hot cross buns have long been popular in both
Great Britain and the United States. The buns are
sweet rolls filled with raisins. They are marked
with a cross made from sugar frosting.

At first, hot cross buns were baked and eaten
only on Good Friday. But they became so popular
that now they are baked all through Lent. People
in other countries bake many different kinds of
Easter breads and cakes.

For the Easter meal, many families have ham. Ham is smoked pork that comes from pigs. In many countries the pig is a sign of good luck and wealth. That is why small banks are often piggy banks.

In some countries, especially Italy, Greece, and parts of the Middle East, the Easter meat is roast lamb.

The Easter walk is an old custom. After Easter services in the Middle Ages, townspeople in their finery walked from church into the fields.

The Easter walk lives on in the Easter parades that are held in many cities. In New York City, thousands of people turn out to see crowds walking down Fifth Avenue. In London, the Easter Parade is held in Battersea Park.

42

For a long time, people have worn new clothes on Easter. In fact, some people think that it is bad luck not to wear at least one new piece of clothing. On Easter Sunday many women wear a new hat—an "Easter bonnet."

In earlier times, a young man would send a pair of gloves to his sweetheart. This was a proposal of marriage. If she accepted his offer, she wore the gloves on Easter morning.

Early people thought that nature itself took part in Christ's death and resurrection. People believed that darkness covered the earth as Christ hung on the cross. They also believed that the sun danced as it rose in the sky on Easter morning.

44

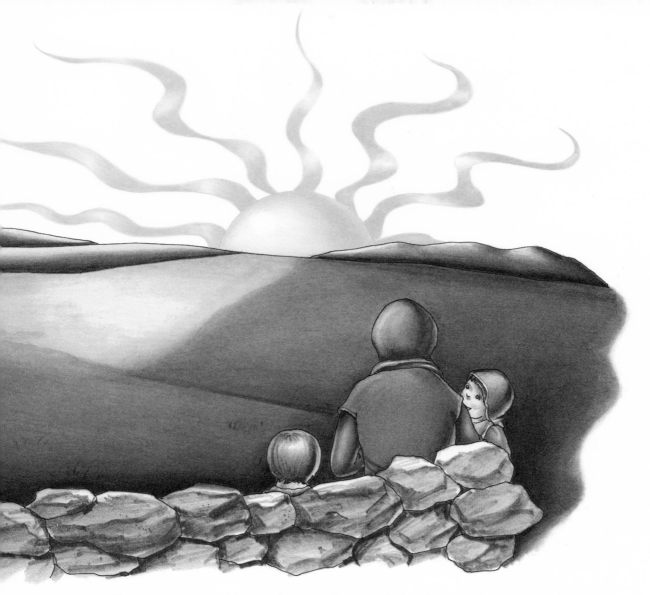

Sometimes people gathered before dawn in an open field to watch the sunrise. Often at dawn, the sun's rays do look like they are dancing.

The rising sun is a sign of newness and hope. Some people still go outdoors early Easter morning. Sunrise services are very popular.

Churches all over the world hold services on Easter morning. Bells ring and people sing joyful hymns. The word **Alleluia** (all-ay-LOO-yuh) is often heard. This means "Praise God." Because of Christ's resurrection, Christians are filled with hope and joy.

Easter is an important religious holiday, but it is more than that. It is a time for everyone to be glad. Decorated eggs, Easter baskets, and lilies are all signs of Easter. They show the joy of life in the coming of springtime and in the rebirth of nature.

INDEX